The 20 steps Diet Debt
How to get out of debt
and Stay Away Forever

To my readers and my wife

Table of Contents

WHY DO YOU NEED TO GET OUT OF DEBT?

Well, I'll give you 5 reasons.

1) Everything you buy becomes much more expensive

You don't believe me? Ok, let's see with an example.

You really want to buy a new plasma television. The price was $2300, but it has been reduced to $1995.
Probably you'll think that a bargain price, so you sign up to an "attractive looking" credit agreement

But, **do you know how much will it cost?**

Did you answer $1995?

You're wrong!

Every time you borrow to buy something, the total cost is composed by three distinct parts.

a) The actual amount that is borrowed: $1995

b) The interest on the loan. Probably 3 years at 29.9% APR. So that will cost approx. $915

c) These payments must be made from your taxed income. Probably 30% of tax. That would add approx. $1250

Let's do the sum... **The total cost is: $4160**! It's more than the double basic price! Just for a Television.

So do you still think that's a bargain price? Do you really want this television?

2) Lack of Freedom

There are too many peoples who have a "must have" attitude. But if they can't afford their desires, the "must have" attitude translates into a "must borrow" attitude

This type of attitude is not without consequences. Every time you borrow money, you link you to a financial institution, you give it a part of your life and the lender owns a bit of you. Every month you are paying your loan, you are repaying your freedom.

The more you lower your debt, the more you raise your freedom. It's a simple equation.

3) Rows

What is the most common reason of problems in couple? Is it for the sex? Because the children? Or because the lack of cleaning the house?

No, you're wrong!

It's for money. Debt is the first cause of relationship problems.

4) Stress

It's inevitable. You owe money that you no longer have and you have to repay it plus the interest. You'll work to repay it and make ends meet. Every time, there is a doubt in your mind "what if... I can't keep up?"

Moreover, there is a huge frustration of being chained with debt.

5) Bankruptcy

Yeah, there is always a risk of Bankruptcy. One debt can lead to another debt.

For some people, after they borrowed money once, it's more and more easy to borrow money. Beware of this type of behavior.

It's easy to say "oh stick it on my credit card" but it's really more difficult to repay, especially with a huge interest rate.

Eventually, it can get to the stage where you can't even afford to repay the interest, let alone the original amount you borrowed.

I think, now you have enough reasons to get out of debt.

THE 20 STEPS DIET DEBT

The most important in this journey is to know that your debt will not disappear within a week.

So, here we go with the 20 steps.

STEP 1: YOU HAVE TO DETERMINE EXACTLY HOW MUCH DEBT YOU HAVE

It's the first step, all next steps are depending of this. If you don't know the amount of your debt, you won't be able to start your journey to get out of debt.

How can you do that?

It's simple, **collect all your credit reports** and sum up everything.

Don't be afraid, it can be a lot of money, but no worries you will be free of debt. .

STEP 2: STOP MAKING UNNECESSARY EXPENSES

It's probable you grab a soda and/or a coffee at work every day. You can think that it's nothing, that's just a few bucks. But they can quickly add up!

Try to make a list of those expenses and add up the total, I'm pretty sure that you'll be surprised.

Now, just imagine a way to cut off all of those expenses.

Here are some ideas to save money:

- bring your lunch to work, stop buying them at a restaurant near your work
- cancel your cable or cell phone service or if you can't live without get the cheapest plan available
- Try to carpool, to catch the subway or bus to go to work
- Try to use coupons when buying groceries or shop at wholesale stores

At the end of the month, you'll see that you saved a lot of money.

You probably work 20 days a month, so you have 20 lunches at work and you probably buy 20 lunches at work.

In New York, one lunch cost $15. At the end of the month you'll save $300. Yes 2 hundred. And now, per year, you work 220 days probably, so do the math, you can save $3,300 per year.

Ok, but you'll tell me "I need to eat for lunch! It costs money!". A brown bag lunch cost 3$. The differential cost is $12.

Again let's do the math, for one year, you can save $2,640. It's pretty cool isn't it?

STEP 3: MAKE YOUR HOMEWORK. LEARN

ABOUT THE CREDIT CARDS YOU HAVE

Did you read all the contracts you've signed? Did you know how the interests are calculated? The best way to prevent credit card debt is by knowing how your credit card works.

When you're approved for a credit card, you're given a line of credit, which is typically the maximum balance you can accumulate on the card.

The average interest rate is 20 %. Yes. 20%.

Try with an example. You buy something at $100, at the end you have to pay it $120.

Do you really want to give 1/5 of the price to your creditor?

I engage you to read the small lines about minimum payment, and what it does reimburse first. Sometimes the minimum payment reimburse only the rates and the fees, it doesn't reimburse the capital. Surprising isn't it? With a minimum payment, you can reimburse forever.

Yes. In general, a minimum payment, credit card companies have to use to pay down your highest interests balance first.

STEP 4: STOP SPENDING BAD HABITS

Yes, it looks like the step 2, but it's a little different. It's a behavior, it's making a commitment.

It's pretty easy to say "it's ok, stick it on my credit card", but do you really need to make this expense? Did you realize that you will have to pay it, and more than the price showed?

Behavioral economist Meir Statman, said "getting out of debt is the financial equivalent of trying to quit smoking."

It's Just like any bad habit, only good intentions won't be enough. To ensure success, you need to break your underlying patterns of behavior

It takes 3 weeks to develop a habit and make it normally. You have to make it as a routine. Every day, you'll do it. Each week it will get easier and easier.

STEP 5: DEVELOP YOUR OWN BUDGET

A budget is a document, like a piece of paper or an excel file. In it you will allocate money to the right expenses.

How to do it?

Make a list of all your expenses, including holidays, birthdays, debts you owe, transportation costs, etc.

How to build a Day to Day Budget?

1) Step 1: Track all your expenses

We've seen that you have to make a list of all your expenses during a year.

You have to estimate all your costs: your housing costs, food, utilities, clothing, medical expenses, family expenses, transportation and vehicle costs, entertainment and activities, payment debts priorities, other expenses and saving for in case of emergency.

Since it's down, you have to structure it:

2) Step 2: Structure your budget

Ok, now you have a huge list. Putting it down under categories will improve it a lot.

Make two columns, one with the categories you've listed, and put in front of them the total amount.

You'll have something like this:

Expenses	Total
Housing	
Food	
Utilities	
Clothing	
Medical	
Family	
Transports	
Activities	
Holidays	
Debts	
Saving	
Total	

3) Step 3: Don't forget to monitor and review your budget

Your budget should be flexible, and to be flexible you have to make reviews from time to time. If you don't review it, you'll lose with it.

4) Step 4: Keep being well informed

There are tons of budgeting tips, tools and information on the Internet, you have to know what is a credit, how it works, what is a medical insurance, did you find the right one for your needs? And so on.

5) Step 5: Make budgeting a happy activity

To make your budget doesn't have a painful activity and the sign of a lot of restrictions. The budgeting process will make new habits and you'll know where your money is going.

It can be a game, to optimize your expenses, to try to increase your saving, etc.

STEP 6: FIND A WAY TO INCREASE YOUR INCOME

You can find that step pretty obvious. But when you will develop your budget, it's probable that you'll realize that you don't make enough money to pay for all of your expenses and debts. To find an extra income doesn't mean having to get a second job, it can mean changing your lifestyle. Why not trying to use public transports instead of your car?

Here it goes a list of ways to increase your income:

- Start to sell on eBay
- If you have crafting skills, start to sell on Etsy
- You have a good writing skill? You can be a part time freelancer for creative writing or copy writing
- You play well piano or guitar? Put an ad for some lessons
- There is no limit, take a moment, find an activity/hobby you like and start to monetize it.

STEP 7: DEVELOP YOUR BATTLE PLAN TO GET OUT OF DEBT

No readymade plan will save you. You have to make your own plan and prioritizing your debt.

Examine in details all of your debts and determine which debt you have to pay off first.

Two things to know:

- Pay the credit with the highest rate first
- If two credits have the same balance, pay off the smallest.

If you followed the previous steps, I'm pretty sure that you have saved some money (with lunch, and so on) and earn some more money.

Don't spend it.

Use the ¾ of this amount to reimburse your debts, set aside the rest on a saving account for emergencies (see the step 18). It will prevent you to use your credit cards.

Write down your plan, put it in a place you can see it every day and keep it in made, don't make shortcuts!

STEP 8: DETERMINE WHY YOU SPEND MONEY AND TRY TO CHANGE IT

It's probable, that you made unnecessary purchases when you are feeling depressed or angry. It's also possible that you are an impulse buyer.

You have to expenses. But there is always a way to change this attitude.

Every time you make a sacrifice and stay on your budget, you are investing in your future. Always keep that in mind.

The fastest you get out of debt, the more money you'll have.

Step 9: Pay On Time

You have to always make payments on time for all your debts. If you do that, you will never fall in the debt trap (moreover, this tip can also help you keep your financial situation intact).

Your financial obligations won't disappear if you put it under the carpet. It will be worse and worse. Penalties and other fees can make a really big amount of money at the end. Don't try to escape.

If you're struggled, call your creditors and try to negotiate with them.

STEP 10: PAY WITH CASH

Paying with cash is a good way to don't spend money in useless objects.

Take your cards out of your wallet, store them in a place that is not easily accessible and do not let others know where you have hidden them.

When you'll get in some shopping, with only $20 or $100 with no credit card, you will not have the easy way "stick it on my credit card". Yes, it can be a little frustrating, but you spent only cash you had in your pocket, not virtual cash you didn't owned.

STEP 11: SELL SOME ITEMS

Selling some unused assets can be a good source of extra cash. You can sell:

- Some jewelry,

- your second car,

- old clothes,

- hi-fi,

- some books,

- and so on, this list had no end.

STEP 12: SOME OF YOUR FRIENDS COULD BE BAD FOR YOUR DEBT

If you've made some shopping with your friends, you have certainly notices that some of them encourage you to spend more heavily than other of your friends.

Some of them say to you easily "stick it on your credit card, because you deserve it"

Moreover, when people go shopping together they tend to encourage each other to spend more money that they don't have.

If you were alone, you wouldn't purchase that expensive thing. But your friend said "oh that's nice!" and you've instantly wanted it and you bought it.

If you want to improve your financial situation, there is an easy answer: stop shopping with them. I don't want you that you don't see them, just to stop making shopping with them.

Finally, but not the last, keep in mind that the mantra: 'Oh, I've lost my job/I'm angry/I'm depressed, I think I'll go and spend money to make me feel happier'. Is not an answer.

If you experience these feelings, get a punching ball and try to destroy it, instead of wasting your money.

STEP 13: DON'T TRUST THE RULES OF YOUR CREDITORS: PAY MORE THAN THE MINIMUM

The most important lesson you can learn about getting out of debt is:

You'll NEVER get out of debt if you play by the rules of your creditors. No matter what they say, they really don't want you to get out of debt.

Why? Because the longer it takes you to pay off your debt, the more money they'll make.

You'll NEVER get out of debt by just making minimum payments.

So, pay more than the minimum payment per month.

Step 14: Negotiate your debt

How do you pay off your credit card bills? When you have the money, right?

Make a debt settlement with your creditors.

Work out an agreement with them, renegotiate the interest rates and the amount if you can pay your bill more quickly.

But this method needs to be accurate on payments and a higher income, than usual. So if you don't meet the requirements, you can take a consolidation loan.

STEP 15: CLOSE THE ACCOUNTS YOU DON'T

NEED ANYMORE

Two rules:

1) Have maximum 3 credit cards.

2) Close all your store cards. If you need to buy something, than use your credit card and pay it off at the end of the month.

Do you really think that you need 7 credit cards and 5 store cards? Did you calculate all the fees you pay just by keep them in your wallet?

STEP 16: SHOP SMART

You can buy at discounted price, buy online, use coupons, etc.

Here is a list of 14 tips about smart shopping:

- Avoid the mall, go to specialty stores

- Make a list and STICK on it: buy what you need, not what you want

- Create a shopping budget (see the step 5)

- Set a timeframe that you will complete your shopping in, once that time is over, it's time to go home

- Never go shopping the last two weeks before Christmas

- Shop alone, don't shop with your friends (see the step 12)

- Buy on sale, buy at discounted price

- Use coupons

- But don't buy because it's on sale

- Buy online

- Choose quality over quantity. Yes you'll pay a bit more, but you won't have to rebuy the same things two weeks after because it was poor made.

- Try dollar stores and thrift stores

- Ask "Do I really need this?"

- Don't shop when you are tired, hungry, lonely or bored (see the step 4)

STEP 17: KEEP THE CHANGE

Yes, save coins. All of them. If you follow the step 10, at the end of the day, you find some coins in your pockets.

For today, perhaps it's not too much, but day after day, the amount will grow, more than you ever imagined.

In one year, I filled 4 jam jars, it's pretty heavy, it takes up space, but it grants some extra cash!

STEP 18: OPEN A SAVING ACCOUNT IN CASE OF EMERGENCY.

If you start saving on a monthly or a daily basis, your savings can amount to a lot of money.

For example if you save $150 on a monthly basis, in one year you will save $1800.

In case of emergency it can prevent you to use your credit card and pay a lot of fees and interests.

And if there is no emergency, you'll saved $1800!

Step 19: Exercise discipline

To get out of debt is not an easy journey, it requires enormous discipline, it could be the toughest thing you'll ever do in your life.

The more you owe, the harder it will.

You have to make a commitment with yourself, not just telling "ok why not, someday I will"

You have to be pulled by the envy of being debt free!

If you still think "really? Why I have to get out of debt?", read again the 5 reasons of the introduction.

To have debts it's a vicious circle, you make one credit, then one more, then… and if you don't be cautious you can fall in bankruptcy.

STEP 20: DEBT CONSOLIDATION LOAN

If you can't negotiate your debt with your creditors, another way is to consolidate your debts into one loan and pay it off with lower monthly installments and a lower interest rate.

There are many different ways to consolidate debt. The most important step in this direction is to shop for the best terms and lowest interest rate.

Usually terms are connected to collateral or what assets you have to secure your loan principal. But, you'd be surprised to discover that terms of collateral can vary even more than interest rates!

To sum up: You need a COMMITMENT and Stick to the plan!

1) Step 1: Start where you are

It's probable that you didn't have look at your financial position since a long time.

But now, you need to draw up an inventory of your personal finance.

How can you do that? It's very easy!

You need a pen, a paper, all your credit card bills, and a high dose of honesty.

Make a list of all your debts and their interest rates and the minimum monthly repayments.

It's normal to be worried about how much you owe, but you can get rid of all your debt within 5-7 years.

2) Step 2: Stop spending more than you earn

Yes. STOP that. Perhaps you like luxurious clothes, perhaps you like to have the newest phone. But if you have to borrow money to buy those objects, stop that.

Look at your living expenses and cut out those things you can't afford.

Moreover, cut up all the credit cards, except one for emergencies.

Make a commitment with yourself: only spend what you can afford.

3) **Step 3: Find some money to pay down your debts**

After sticking to the step 2, the next step is to find some money to start paying down your debts. Pay as much as you can, it's better to pay down your debts than to put your money in a saving account.

Why? Because the interest of your credit is higher than the interest of your saving account. If you put your money in, instead of paying those down, you're losing money.

Choose to pay down the credit with the highest rate first. If you have credits with the same interest rate, pay down the one with the smallest balance first.

4) **Step 4: Build a Savings Fund**

To have your credits under control and pay down them it's a good thing. But don't forget to put some money aside for emergencies. And by putting money aside, you'll start to build some saving and it will boost you to see the amount growing.

5) **Step 5: Pay down That Mortgage.**

It's the last debt you have to take care, the interest rate is a lot lower than any other credit.

www.ingramcontent.com/pod-product-compliance
Lightning Source LLC
Chambersburg PA
CBHW070721180526
45167CB00004B/1569